This is What I Feel, and I'm not Apologising

Amy Pryor

BookLeaf Publishing

This is What I Feel, and I'm not Apologising

Presentation by *BookLeaf Publishing*

Web: www.bookleafpub.com

E-mail: info@bookleafpub.com

ISBN: 9789357211796

First edition 2023

DEDICATION

To anyone who may be able to relate, this is for you.

ACKNOWLEDGEMENT

Thank you Ellie Pearson and Paris Rodriguez for your support and encouragement through this process - this wouldn't exist without you.

Happiness

Everyone, and I mean everyone, wants to
achieve happiness.
It's a multi-million-dollar industry now, with
so called professionals giving advice, telling you
what to do and
how to do it.
You all want it, don't even try to convince me
that you don't;
but have you actually thought about what is it?
Seriously, what is it?
Wait! Don't tell me.
I can't have you all shouting at once, and then
getting aggravated when you realize people have
a different answer.
Because that's what we do isn't it? We defend
our meaning of the word
happiness.
But, you're all actually wrong on what it is.
Don't hate me, it's true.
You can all tell me things that bring you
happiness, because that's all it is;
happiness is simply an
emotion,
one of many,
not a goal.

You want to achieve happiness? Well
congratulations, you already have.
You are born with the ability to feel happy.
So, what is it that you want?
Because it's not happiness, we just established
this.
You need to find a new goal, one that will make
you
happy.
But when that feeling of happiness is replaced
with something else, it doesn't mean you have
failed.
You can feel happiness again, just like you will
feel that other emotions again.
Emotions aren't a goal; they are just a part of
life.
So, what's your new goal?
I hope it's better
than happiness.

Autism

Autism.
Bet that's something you can't really
comprehend.
Don't worry, you're not alone.
Everyone who doesn't have it has a
false idea of what is it. And even if you do have
it, there's no
guarantee you understand it either. Let's get one
thing straight; even though we need extra
help sometimes, that doesn't mean we're broken
I am not broken.
Just because I may not see things the same as
you, doesn't mean I am not your
'kind'. If you
lend me your hand and compassion,
maybe we can understand this together. I'm
not going to lie, autism isn't something I'm
overly educated in. But,
please show me some patience, my brain isn't
quite the same as yours, but
really that doesn't make me who I am. You must
see that autism doesn't define me. I'm
totally
unique, but that's because of a

variety of reasons. Please don't view me as just one thing.

Would you see a returned solider as the Xanax they are prescribed to cope? Or would you realize that doesn't make them who they are? So while I may display a little more zeal than someone else, I promise that I am normal too.

Loneliness

There's one thing worse than bullies
and that's friends who ignore you.
Isolate, or make fun of
and put you down too.

Of course they say they're joking,
it's always in good fun.
But one day you will stop and think,
'what have I actually done?'

They don't mean to do this
but they make you feel so bad.
To you this is perfectly normal;
isn't that kind of sad?

You don't really question it
as you sit alone in class.
But it's like everyone looks through you,
just a wall made of glass.

You sit there and wonder what you did,
just constantly asking why.
But you have to try to hold it together
they can't see you cry.

There's a wall between you and your friends,
it keeps pushing you back.
You want to shout out to your friends,
ask them to cut you some slack.

Your friend turns around to talk to you;
a slow smile spreads across your face.
But she says 'you need to lighten up',
you feel that closes the case.

Your friends don't know as you ask yourself,
'what have I done wrong?'
Then you come to the conclusion
'maybe I just don't belong'.

Please stop, and listen

Stop.
Just stop, and listen.
You can do that, right? Don't judge or stare or laugh or try to understand;
you don't need to understand,
just listen.
I have something to tell you. But it's hard. I can't get the words out I'll stumble and stutter and freeze and break and
… breathe.
Just breathe.
I have something to tell you. I haven't told anyone.
I guess it's not really a secret because I mean it doesn't really matter it's not special and I don't want anything to change just listen.
Why aren't you listening?!
… I'm sorry. I have something to tell you.
It's about me.
Maybe you've guessed, I don't know.
Maybe it's not a secret; I guess it doesn't really matter.
But it's the truth, and I can't hide it. Not anymore.
I shouldn't have to.

But I will.
I need to tell you, though.
So please, just listen.
I promise it won't take long.
Please stop
and listen.

I'm sorry

I sorry I disappoint you,
I'm sorry I bring you shame.
I'm sorry I make you flinch,
whenever you hear my name.

I'm sorry I'm not the daughter
you always thought I'd be.
I'm sorry that being myself
makes you so unhappy.

I'm sorry I'm not the same,
how I can't love who you want me to.
I'm sorry I'm the odd one out;
I'm not the same as you.

I'm sorry that I am different
I've tried my best to change.
You don't know what it's like
being trapped inside this cage.

Staying at home is awkward
going to school makes it worse.
Isn't it said to think
that I can't escape this curse?

My friends question everything I do;
they kicked me out that day.
I'm not sure what I'm meant to do
what more can I say?

I leave home and am constantly judged,
I return to a world of hate.
Can you just try to understand
why I haven't been happy of late?

Just try to imagine what it must be like
to live in constant fear.
If you were to live my life for a day
I wonder if you'd still be here…

I'm sorry I disappoint you,
I'm sorry I bring you shame.
Do you know how much it kills to see
you flinch when you hear my name?

I See You

I see you.
I see you in your room at night
as you lay awake in bed.
I see you as you shy away
from the thoughts within your head.
I see you with your friends at school
as you flash that fake smile.
I see you as you play pretend,
you've been doing it a while.
I see you as you walk to class
and the words they throw your way.
I see you as your friends laugh at you
all the things you wish to say.
I see you as you pass your mirror;
your eyes don't want to look.
I wonder if you see yourself,
as you become buried in that book.

Do you see when you speak with passion,
there's a twinkle in your eye?
Do you see how happy endings
always make you cry?
Do you see that kid in class,
who always looks to you?

Do you see when you are happy,
you make others smile too?

You don't see your own worth
you don't see yourself at all.
You see only the judgement,
and that makes you feel very small.
You seem to have forgotten
what makes you who you are.
If only you really looked at yourself,
I know it'd take you far.

I see you as you hate yourself;
I know those thoughts aren't tame.
I see you for who you truly are
if only you'd do the same.

I will be your sister

I will be your sister;
always right next to you.
If you feel like you are struggling,
I will get you through.

I will be your sister;
I'll pick you up when you're down.
When you feel low into a smile,
we will make that frown.

I will be your sister;
your shoulder when you need to cry.
I'll always listen and support you,
on me you can rely.

I will be your sister;
you're toughest critic out there.
It comes from a place of love,
it's only because I care.

I will be your sister;
I'll always share your joy.
I'll be your loudest supporter,
until it begins to annoy.

I will be your sister;
I don't care if you're not my blood.
My love for you will only grow,
like an opening flower bud.

For a sister is a protector
a counsellor, a mum, a friend.
I will always stick by you
until the very end.

I will be your sister;
no you don't get a say.
I will love you with everything I am
even after you walk away.

Love me, but let me go

My time has come and gone.
It is your job now to remember me, but let me
move on;
Love me, but let me go.
I have left this world to continue this journey of
life.
I go at a heavy price though,
I must leave you behind.
So to make my pain more bearable, I ask you
just one favour;
Love me, but let me go.
Remember me with a smile, think about me with
fondness, love me with everything you have,
but move on.
I will always be with you, but never throw your
life away
just because I'm not there to say 'I love you'.
Because one day, you will join me on the second
part of this journey called
life.
I will be waiting for you. But until then;
Love me, but let me go…

Loss

You hear stories of other people's loss
and you think it won't happen to you.
Until you lose someone you love;
and you realize what they went through.

When you lose someone you love
it's like the world has been turned upside down.
You look around you and wonder,
'How can no one else have a frown?'

Your friends will say it's ok;
'They wouldn't want you to be sad'.
You know this, but can't move on
so you start to feel bad.

You know they'd want you to move on,
'Love me, but let me go'.
But all you can do is cry
because you loved them so.

You can't bare to live a normal life
it's like you've fallen into a hole.
You will eventually climb back out,
but this will take its toll.

Sometimes, as you're walking along
you'll look at the heavens and cry.
You can't understand why they had to leave,
you'll always wonder why.

Eventually, you embrace this grief
it becomes part of who you are.
But you'll never completely close the door on it;
it will always be ajar.

At death's door

You were struggling so much for breath
on that last fateful day.
Every time you stopped your breathing
I thought you'd slipped away.
Tears ran down our cheeks
as you laid on that cold floor.
We knew this was the end
you were at death's door.
My Aunty cried as she kissed you
and she said she loved you so.
You were the greatest father
the only one she wanted to know.
I couldn't bear to say anything
as tears ran down my face.
You took your last breaths
you were finally finishing this race.
Watching you slowly slip away
was the worst pain I have felt.
I was kind of glad your pain would end
as beside you I loyally knelt.
The sight of you lying on that floor
is forever branded in my brain.
It randomly flashes into my mind
making me hunch over in pain.
I felt you there beside me

as I walked onto that stage.
I could feel you cheering me on
laughing at me, I'd wage.
Your mouth is open, your eyes closed;
we know the end is near.
It's time for you to finally go
I'll always hold you dear.

Depression

The thought of being perfect,
is slowly closing in.
It's a fight against society,
which she can never win.

He cannot slip and show his friends,
he is in so much pain.
He continues on with his walls up,
only to go home and cry again.

Her friends criticize what she does,
there's judgment in their eyes.
She just smiles and plays along
not one of them hear her cries.

He feels all alone and wants a friend,
who will take the time to care.
He cannot continue to struggle alone,
he needs someone who won't judge and stare.

She needs to let out her pain,
so she grabs a razor blade.
The physical pain amuses her,
as she laughs at the lines she made.

He's filled with so much darkness,
why can't anybody understand?
He is empty and all alone.
can't anybody lend a hand?

They are all alone and filled with pain,
and anger and grief and loss,
They darkness is slowing killing them;
they need to get this message across.

Tired of putting up with the pain,
she writes a suicide note.
She's drowning in the waters of despair,
and couldn't get back in her boat.

He can't go on like this anymore,
he finds his father's gun.
He points the gun to his head,
it suddenly weighs a tonne.

All of a sudden these two are dead,
their families wondering why.
These two deaths could have been prevented,
if only someone had heard them cry.

What Happened?

Alive. I just want you here with me,
but you had other ideas. I
can't believe that you're gone. Why
didn't you tell me you were unhappy? I didn't
ever think I'd be sitting at your
funeral; you're
gone. You always seemed so
happy, but I guess
I was wrong. I
just want to
know why? What
lead you to that point? I'm sitting with your
mother, your friends, your teammates. Your
Nan wrote a letter, because she couldn't make it,
but your mum can't
open the envelope.
Please tell us what happened. It's so
quiet now.
Really quiet. We can't handle this
silence; it's
tearing our group apart. We can't
understand what went wrong. We thought you
were so
very happy;
we were wrong. Your

x-ray showed your broken neck.
You were so young. You'll never get old; we'll
never see your
zealous self again.

You left me here alone

You're lying on your bed at night
you've barely made it through the day.
Wishing that the pain will end
you'd be dead if you had your way.

Your thoughts give you no mercy
as you lay awake at night.
You hardly get any sleep again
your muscles are bunched up tight.

Spiritually exhausted, you lay there
trying to find the will to get out of bed.
You have no desire to keep going
at this point you're wishing you were dead.

It's impossible to explain to someone
the pain they cannot see.
It's just easier to show the world
that you are 'truly' happy.

As you live your life of lies
you know you can always make this end.
No one said that would be easy
but this thought becomes your friend.

Eventually, you've had enough,
you decide to take your life.
You never stopped to think
how this cuts me like a knife.

You are gone, your pain has stopped
but I am still stuck here.
It was a selfish decision you made,
I'll always hold you dear.

Why did you leave me here all alone?
you knew I always cared!
I was always there when you needed me
when you made both of us scared.

I loved you with everything I had
yet you left me here all alone.
I'm left with a whole full of grief;
if only I'd picked up the phone…

Do you know how hard it was
walking in your room that day?
There is nothing you could do to make it better
there is nothing more to say.

The suicide survivor

Roses are red
violets are blue
I'm reminded everyday
of how much I miss you.

Roses are red
you couldn't do it anymore
you took your own life
I've been through this before.

Roses are red
I'm here yet again
I know why you did it;
you were in too much pain.

Roses are red
we all say you were kind
you had so much to give but,
you couldn't escape your mind.

Roses are red
… no, I'm done.
I don't care what society says
I'm going to run my tongue.

How could you do that to me?
through everything I was there!
I fought so hard to keep you alive
did you even care?

I gave you all my strength,
so what do I do now?
now you've taken centre stage
go ahead, take your bow.

My life is a mess
you threw it into chaos
I gave you everything I had
and now I'm just lost.

There's nothing inside me
I can't even sleep
I can't think straight anymore
I can only just weep.

What do I do now?
everything is gone
I gave my life to you
and now it's all torn.

For the suicide survivor
they give and they give
and when suddenly they don't have to
they forget how to live.

You must feel so empty;
so lost and alone.
Full of such grief
if only you'd picked up the phone.

It's time to put that down now
you've been through enough.
You can admit that it was hard
you don't have to be tough.

For the suicide survivor
ignored themselves for too long.
To focus on their needs now
just feels selfish and wrong.

Roses are red
violets are blue
not a day goes by
where I don't miss you.

I sit here in the darkness

I sit here in the darkness
watching everything go by.
I'm filled with so much pain
That I can't even cry.

I remember the day we met
out there in the sun.
We laughed and talked and played
we had so much fun.

But little did I know
there was darkness in your mind.
As we ran this race called life
you felt very much behind.

I sit here in the darkness
watching everything go by.
I'm filled with so much pain
that I can't even cry.

That day you first told me
of the pain you'd been through.
You buried your head in my shoulder;
I just had to help you.

But now I sit here in the darkness
watching everything go by.
I'm filled with so much pain
that I can't even cry.

It began with text messages
highlighting all your pain.
I was happy for you to talk
if it could keep you sane.

And then came the phone calls
I was trying to keep you here.
You'd had enough you wanted out
but I held you too dear.

On and on it went
a battle I didn't choose.
Yet I had to keep fighting;
I couldn't afford to lose.

Yet now I sit here in the darkness
watching everything go by.
I'm filled with so much pain
that I can't even cry.

I'm the reason you finally left
on that dark and lonely night.
I'm so sorry I wasn't there
as you extinguished your little light.

I just couldn't take it anymore
and so I turned off my phone.
I missed your calls and made you
feel very much alone.

So now I sit here in the darkness
watching everything go by.
I deserve this pain I feel
as I finally begin to cry.

A girl in a cage

She stands apart from the others, stuck inside her
cage.
Her coffin.
She can never be like them
and oh
how she envies them.
What was done to her
what she still goes through
marks her as different.
She wants to talk to people; smile and make a
joke or just say 'have a good day'. But they'll
see the
label
that has been branded upon her,
and walk away.
And there stands in the corner,
another girl in a cage.
With her limpless hair and her
empty eyes;
as if she has no will to
hold herself upright.
She looks up. Their gazes lock, and you'd think
something would
happen.
A smile

a wave
an understanding.
Nothing.
Just an awareness.
An awareness of knowledge;
one of them won't be making it through the night.

I'm okay.

What do you mean, I'm not fine?

I'm not trying to argue here, I just don't understand.
I manage fine all the time; you want to lend a hand?
Ok, I'm shaking all the time, but I sleep enough a day
to at least be able to function; that's not normal you say?
I don't want to be here, but I still get out of bed
are you saying it's not ok, to constantly fight against your head?
I'm pushing down the painful thoughts, so I'm not about to cry.
You're telling me it's not normal, to not care if you die?
I'm eating, sleeping and functioning; isn't that enough?
To me that's perfectly normal, I'm not trying to be tough.
Ok, I guess if it were you, that would give me cause to worry.
But it's not you we're talking about; it doesn't count for me.

To me this is normal, as I live my life of lies.
Telling myself I'm fine, has become my greatest disguise.
I've been telling myself this for so long, I can't just let it end.
I need your help pointing it out, your patience you'll have to lend.
I'm sorry I cause you such worry, as my thoughts I start to share;
I'm used to people not batting an eye, I'm not used to those who care.
Thank you, my friend, for seeing me, for seeing that I'm not fine.
Convincing myself I'm ok, has made my health decline.

But seriously though, I'm okay…

Candle

Imagine you have a candle, held tightly in your hand.
Everything around you is darkness, a strange and foreign land.
You know if you let your candle blow out, you'll have nothing left at all.
The darkness reaches out to claim you, you can almost hear its call.
There are other lights around you, you know others are there.
But as your candle slowly goes out, it's hard for you to care.
You are utterly exhausted, as you keep your candle alight.
It's all you can focus on, but you're starting to lose the fight.
The darkness gets harder to fight, as someone's light goes out;
'How dare you add to my darkness', is all you want to shout.
But as your body begins to shake, from the struggle with your flame.
You get why they let it go out; your despair you have to tame.

For when you focus on your struggles, is when
your candle burns low.
Darkness reaches out to claim you, circling like
a crow.
How can you focus on anything else, when this
takes all your will?
You can't focus on your pain; all you can do is
hold still.
Keeping your flame alight, is everything you
are.
Maybe there's life around you, but you can't
look that far.
Then someone comes up to you, and says you're
not okay.
But how can you think of that, as you struggle
day by day?
Apparently keeping your flame alight, does not
make you fine.
Your definition of ok, is not the same as mine.
Maybe I'm not ok, maybe I'm almost gone;
will I let my light go out, to this darkness I am
drawn.

Exhaustion

I wake up, struggling for breath.
I remember the dream.
The pain that I felt, the pain that I feel
in my head
in my heart
in my soul.
Were they dreams, or were they memories
or were they memories made dreams?
Am I even awake now?
I woke up in my dream so many times
I don't even remember what's real.
The feelings are real though
and the pain in my stomach as it clenches and
I'm sent to the toilet
yet again.
Was it real?
Is my friend alright?
Did I do that?
I need to check on them!
But it's 3 o'clock in the morning
I have to wait for hours in agony
wondering if the horrors were real.
I sit here in the darkness
too scared to move
even as the blood drips from my nose

terrified of what I might do.
Am I dreaming now? Maybe I am and the
images before were the memories
or maybe I'm still asleep, and I just woke up in
my dream again.
Who knows
I can't remember anymore.
I'm slowly losing my mind.
The pain, the agony, the confusion, sending me
from my bed with my stomach bunched tight
making me fear the worst, fear for my loved
ones, fear myself.
What have I done?
If this is real, if I'm awake, then this pain and
not knowing is worse than the dream itself.
It's a terrifying reality to live in
even if it isn't real.
And you want me, to go back to sleep?

Nothing

Someone once said to me
"What's the worst emotion you can feel?"
I thought for a minute, and I thought some more
and I said:

Well, it could be grief, where something was
lost.
It takes your innocence; there's no greater cost.
It could be guilt, where something wasn't done.
The weight of that guilt; it definitely weighs a
tonne.
Then there's regret, now that one's crap.
All the 'what ifs'; it becomes an endless trap.
Envy, sadness, rage; there's so many you see?
To pick just one…
But I know what it will be.
It slowly creeps upon you, you don't hear its
call.

See, the worst feeling
is when you don't feel
anything
at all."

Broken.

Broken.
Every part of me, has been
broken
destroyed.
There is no part
left
that hasn't been completely
shattered.
The pieces don't fit together
anymore;
they are too jaggered and
raw
have been burnt
broken
destroyed
can never be put back together
they don't make a human.
I am not human.
I am nothing but pain.
That's all I feel
that's all I know
that's all I bring.
I didn't do this to myself
this has been done
to me

and now all I can do
is do the same to others.
Maybe it would be better
if I just
go.

www.ingramcontent.com/pod-product-compliance
Lightning Source LLC
Chambersburg PA
CBHW051741130826
49812CB00033B/949
* 9 7 8 9 3 5 7 2 1 1 7 9 6 *